A Work in
Progress!!!

Trying to find Love!!!

Lessons on Losing, Gaining and

Surviving Love!!!

WRITTEN BY CLARA V. CHARITY

The Reading Glass Books
(888) 420-3050
www.readingglassbooks.com
production@readingglassbooks.com

What this book is about!!

Showing women and men that you must go through things in your life to make you a better person for you! This book is very special to me because it has been my guide to being truly happy in my own life while on my journey to find love.

If you always have things easy, then you can never learn the real process of working to find something that is just meant for you. Being able to find out about how to survive love and being in an abusive relationship. Overcoming the basic things that create a toxic relationship. Knowing when to walk away from someone who is not treating you right.

In order to find real love, you will sometimes have to Lose it, Gain it and Survive it in order to appreciate it when it comes.

Nothing is ever easy but, in the end, it is so worth it....

The Dedication Page

I wrote this book with people in mind who have been in bad relationships and thinking that they can never be happy. There will come a time in your life that you will meet the right person and fall in love and truly understand what it means to be in love with someone that loves you back. It took me many years and many failed attempts at meeting people and learning that we were not a good fit at that time but now I am in a place where I feel nothing but pure love.

There is nothing special about how I feel about falling in love with someone and being in love with that person. It took a strong man to come into my world and choose to love me and I waited a very long time to see it happen and experience what it really feels like to have pure joy. I chose to write about this topic because I have lived it myself and I am only able to tell you what I know and have learned.

The great thing about my new relationship is that I know when that person really loves everything about who you are as a person and funny to say that you complete each other in a lot of ways that make you both so very happy.

Love is so real to me now that I find it funny to feel this way after all this time in my life of being alone. I like I tell others, Embrace the love and enjoy it because this is your time to shine..

The Acknowledgements

The entire point to a Work in Progress is to be searching for something that you never feel like you are going to find. Well just when I got to the point that I was not going to look anymore, I was found by this awesome many who has chosen to make me his wife and spend the rest of his life with me.

There really was a time that I would be alone and angry because I could not find what I saw so many other people around me enjoying. I wanted to be happy and in love too. I had to learn patients with myself and with others because just because someone comes into your life that does not mean that they are meant to be there forever.

My goal was always to find my forever love rather than someone for the moment. When the time came that I stopped looking, I was finally found by my forever love.. The end point of having grace and mercy over your own life is the greatest gift in the world to me and I am happy...

Table of Contents

The Start—Stage 1

In the beginning of every new relationship there is ups and downs that we must endure. This is how we find out if this person is going to be a big impact in our lives or just a momentary thing that is going to teach us a valuable lesson in the end. The first meeting us always the toughest to get through and once that has happened you start to let your guard down to get comfortable with this person. When you first meet someone the look into their eyes can give you goose bumps or scare you to death.

The start of any new love is going to be hard to understand but it will be worth the wait once you get the challenged of finding love, understanding love, and keeping your heart open to real love. When you first meet someone, it feels weird because you don't know anything about each other. But when you sit down and talk to a person and really learn to listen, this is when you can read between the lines of what is being said to you and what they really mean for you to hear and understand.

For the burden of finding love and knowing that someone can love you the way that you feel you deserve to be loved is a different task to take on. In the long run you will see that the true goal is to love yourself and be able to share that love with someone who comes into your life and makes them feel special too. If you love yourself then the rest will find you. If you are ready to give love a try, don't run for the hills the first time something goes wrong because you may lose out on a great partner, friend, lover, but most of all your future mate.

In the start of any relationship, you must get to know the person that you meet and find out if you have a connection. To find a love in someone who has been hurt and seen awful things in their life is a hard pill to swallow for anyone. But think of being in that situation and it is you that have found someone who has been broken and damaged like yourself and you want to try to fix that person. All you can do is love them until they get past the hurt and pain that they have been through. This can apply to both men and women because I have seen many damaged men in my life that had no idea why they did the things that they did or do the things that they do.

Time will come in your relationship that you will have to talk about the past and go over the things that made you who you have become. Sometimes the talks are easy and sometimes they can be very hard, but they are very necessary to build a trusting place for both of you to grow. We all make mistakes but don't define a person because there is a hiccup in the start of things. Remember that this is new for the both of you and you have to give a person a chance before you run away from them.

There are going to be good days and bad days, but you must stay true to yourself and allow your feelings and emotions to come to the surface so that you can address them and then deal with them and decide on what to do next. When you can sit and have a full conversation with someone then you can get a fill for what they are looking for and what they want.

You might find someone, or they find you and you fall for each other and have an awesome conversation and then you realize that there is a special connection between you and now you must figure out if you want to act on it to see where things can go for you both. I have found that you can never know when this is coming into your life. Everyone serves a purpose but there will be only one true person that has a mission to love you the way that you truly deserve.

In love there will always be that overwhelming feeling of if you are doing the right thing and if you are the one for them and them the one for you. You must stop second guessing yourself and just learn to put one foot in front of the other and love. Don't allow your past to define your future because you will never be happy.

Love is a very strong word and a very powerful tool in this crazy world that we live in. However, if you allow yourself to overcome the hurt and pain that you have been through in the past then your new love can be the greatest gift in the world for you and them. When someone tells you that they love you, take your time to understand what comes into play with this phrase.

I LOVE YOU!!! Is a common word that people use but don't understand what it means? Love is something that you will feel for someone who is treating your good. Saying I love you is something that many people can tell you and not really know what it means to say it to you. Love is something that you will be able to see in the actions. People will use the word I love you, but they really don't understand what comes with it. I speak! Don't tell me, show me...

Your past Is the past and you must learn to leave it there to move into something more loving and more special. When you see that there is someone out there for you and who can love you and make you happy then you will understand that the word is at your feet and when it is your time to be happy, you will be.

Time will seem to stand where you are looking out over a dark cloud of hurt and pain. Then you will see the sun come up over the shadow of darkness and then that glimpse of light will hit your face and you will begin to see that your time is not to be happy.

It is very overwhelming to know that most of your life has been spent taking care of everyone around you and no one even thought that you needed someone to take care of you. I have loved and had to learn to love myself to get to a happy place of peace. It has been a very love road and I can honestly say that my life is not the best place in the world, but I am learning to love me first. Over the course of the past few years, I have had to learn to put myself first and make moves to get motivated in new ways that will allow me to see a different and better situation coming into my life.

If you are going through these things in your relationship then maybe you need to sit back and evaluate what is going on and then see if being with this person is really what you want for your life.

The main goal is to find goals that are going to get you back on track and see to it that you are going to get the knowledge of not being abused and taken for granted. In my past experience I have learned that not all that looks good is good and unfortunate for me, I had to learn a hard lesson in a short period of time. I lived the life of an alcoholic and drug user and never got the feeling that most people get. I didn't do those things, but I had the man in my life that destroyed a good thing because he wouldn't stop doing these things..

I never drank or used drugs but I may have well had done it for all the pain that I went through trying to get away from it! The purpose of getting help is so that you don't blame yourself for what is someone else's fault and let them get the best of your mind, soul and most of all you thought of living.

I have chosen to put my experience into a book for others to read because I feel that what I went through so many women and your girls have been there and not all of them were able to pull out of it like I did. I had a great back support system and I never want to go back to that life again, but I know that I look at my own children and I never want them to suffer in their lives like I did in mine.

I chose to get involved with a man that I thought I really knew but in the end I never really knew him at all and most of all I didn't know myself that well either. But it does not work that way and the world is not going to be a better place unless you wake up and decide that life is worth living, and that you have to fight for what you want out of it. If you leave the choices up to someone else then you get left out in the cold, if you choose to fight for what you want then you make your own path and keep going until you get to your goals.

I have been fighting for a long time and I now can see that if I had given up then my life would have been over. I am not a looser I am a fighter and a winner and I achieve whatever I set my mind to do. You can do the same thing if you want it bad enough. If you can find the way to get the goals accomplished then don't let anything get in your way of doing it and getting it done.

It started off a good marriage, but then I did what women have done for ancient time, I tried to make it work for the sake of being married. I fell in love with him but I could not help him and I was not strong enough at that time to let him go without a fight. And a fight is just what I got all the time. He would hit me and I would hit back and it would turn into a brawl between husband and wife. It finally got to the point that my life was worth more than what he could give me and I chose to leave.

I was not going to go down without a fight but now I wish I had left sooner. We never made it too our one year anniversary, he went to jail and I went and filed papers for a divorce. It was finally over and I could work on putting my life back in order. So I thought. I never really thought about how hard things were going to be for me as a single mother with children to raise and the effect it would have on them in the long run. In the process of the abuse, I lost my home, a brand new car and half of my friends. My family never knew what I was going through except my parents and my life was turned upside down for the sake of LOVE!!!!

I was not able to get close to people and when I did he made sure that they ran away. He never wanted anyone to be too close for fear that they would find out what was going on in our marriage. And the sad thing is that for those people who knew what was going on thought it was ok. If you married him, then you had to know what he was doing and how things would end up... If you feel that your mate is going to get away, then you don't have enough trust and faith in your relationship to allow him/her to be him/her own person. Sometimes in life, we get into situations that may make us feel that we have no control, but in the end. The control is all yours.

I for the life of me can't understand why the members of the family that knew what was going on never tried to help fix it, but with the few that didn't know it hurt them to see that I had gone through this nightmare all alone.

They could not understand why I let this happen, or how I allowed it to happen to me and since I was always the strong one for everyone around me but now I was in trouble and no one could help me. I would look at them and never let them down in times of need. I had to find myself all over again because I never believed that the problem was him, it was all on me until one day I woke up to see that God said, "This is not the life I want for you my child". When he came into my life he found a week spot, I was just getting over loosing the father to my child, he had walked out on us and I was feeling alone and unwanted. But it is funny to me now that I look back and I did not feel that way at that time.

My daughter was and still is my life. She was a gift from above and I cherish her every day. My family is now stronger and wiser that we can see the changes in our lives and since the divorce we have all moved on to bigger and better things. I have two books under my belt, I am almost finished with my BA in Business and I am so proud of myself for accomplishing the things that I always wanted to do for myself..

There were times when people would come to me and say that "How could you let that happen to you"? And my response has been, I never saw it coming. I was blind by love and being alone and that is something that I never wanted to be. LONELY!!!! If I had a chance to have a great man in my life and know that he loves me and would be faithful to me then I would jump at the chance for that, but now I am more reluctant to just settle for anything that comes my way. I have come to some conclusions that my life will never settle for second best, because I deserve to be first and on top.... I have learned that in life the one thing that you have to cherish now more than anything is your life and your own heart.

I have had my heart walked on, pushed to the ground, kicked, beat, slapped, and worst of all abused in ways that most women deal with on a daily basis because they feel that they can't get out. Well I am the one woman to tell you that there is hope at the end of the tunnel and you have to want it, look for it, push for it, and most of ask God for it. In my life I can say that without my faith and knowing that I would come out of this mess with my life I would have never made it.

I went to Domestic Violence classes and got help, and I can now admit that it was not me, I was not the one with the problem; I was the one who added to it. I really feel now that it I hadn't gotten the help that I did, I would have committed suicide and ended it all. Sometimes, we as woman think that we can fix everything that comes into our lives bad. This is a myth and it is never going to happen. People can't be fixed. They have to seek help and want to change. If they don't there is nothing that you can do as a wife, girlfriend, mate or anything else that we go by to help men out of that type of behavior.

I feel now that I came alone at a time when someone was needed to carry the burden of taking on the load from the family. When I walked out and finally left, it was the best thing for the both of us, only because he needed help that I could not give to him and I needed help of getting my life back. After all I am only one woman and I can only fight for myself.

I have seen so many women like myself, killed, burned, beaten, and worse scared for life and I can say that I am very lucky that I got out with the scares on the inside and not the outside. My first book was titled "Inside the Heart of a Woman". I am very proud of my work because writing that book allowed me to heal my heart and soul and not allow myself to believe that I was at fault.

At the heart of the first book that I wrote was a very dear friend whom I had met a few years before and he was the one that ended up helping me deal with the pain that I had just come out of and showed me that there is hope for love out there.. He and I are very close till this day, he saved my life the day that he called me to tell me to call the Police and get help...

I have read so many stories of young women and old being mistreated by their mates, spouses, friends, lovers and just the general thought of having someone is not worth your life. If I had come to terms with one thing it is now that I am a better person and when I fall in love again I will make sure that he is going to be good to me and no that he is the one for me and that he is not just going to use me for what he thinks he can take and leave me in a rut.

The past is now dead for me and I am so looking forward to the future of being happy with a great guy and seeing that there is love at that end of the tunnel for me to be happy after abuse. This is my goal for other women, you can overcome abuse and have a better life if you really want that. Don't just say it if you are not ready for it.

When you find yourself at a place in your life where you have the urge to stop living, think about life as if it was all that you have left. If you leave the earth today who would suffer more: Your family, your friends, or the abuser? I have always been one to be a fighter and now I know why. If you give in to your feelings of feeling alone and non-worthy then you will never accomplish anything good. Your basic goal in life is to live it to the fullest of your ability and not waste time dwelling on what happened to you in the past. The past is just that, the past so leave it there and allow yourself to grow and enjoy your future.

If there is something that an abused woman can figure out after the abuse is gone is that she is alive and still has a lot of life to live. If you ask someone who has gone through an abusive relationship what they are glad about "The answer would be that they are still living."

My biggest achievement now is that I can say **I am a survivor**. In life we all have to deal with emotions and hardships that sometimes overwhelm us when we have dealt with pain, there is a way to overcome the pain by finding a way out. Sometimes we need to sit back and look at things from the outside in and see that what we are really looking at is ourselves in the mirror of pain and despair.

The best thing to remember is that there is one chance to seek the help of others in your life. If you give up that chance then you are going to pay the consequences with your life in the end. Is it worth it to do just for love????

Time will seem to stand where you are looking out over a dark cloud of hurt and pain. Then you will see the sun come up over the shadow of darkness and then that glimpse of light will hit your face and you will begin to see that your time is not to be happy.

It is very overwhelming to know that most of your life has been spent taking care of everyone around you and no one even thought that you needed someone to take care of you. I have loved and had to learn to love myself to get to a happy place of peace. It has been a very love road and I can honestly say that my life is not the best place in the world, but I am learning to love me first. Over the course of the past few years, I have had to learn to put myself first and make moves to get motivated in new ways that will allow me to see a different and better situation coming into my life.

Meeting someone and starting a new relationship is hard to do. The world that we live in with social media plays a big role in how you will meet someone. How do you know if that person is good for you? You really don't until you take the time to get to know them. I have chosen to write this book, A work in Progress to show others that being in love, falling in love and losing love is a part of life that everyone must go through before they find that right person for them. There is no such thing as a perfect person but when you meet the love of your life then they are perfect for you.

In the start of meeting someone new, there are going to be fears that you will have to face. These will be past issues that you have to let go of to enjoy what is in front of you. This is going to be a process that is going to take time to understand. When someone comes into your life, there are many ways that things can happen. First thing is you must get to know each other. Second, you spend time together and see if you mesh well with each other's personality and attitudes. Third, you enjoy talking to that person and you have great conversations. With all these things coming together for you both, there should great chemistry. If not, then move on. It is not worth the time and effort that you are going to use because you will know in the beginning if that person is going to be a good match just by talking about different things and spending time with them.

The Intimacy—Stage 2

When someone comes into your life, you feel like you are going to be living a dream. If you allow this to happen when you meet this person you are going to allow yourself to show your soft side to each other and then you can see how far things can go on that first time together. I have been seeing a fact that many people come together and never really know each other.

Intimacy is a gift. Something that should not be taken for granted. To find someone that you can connect with on a mutual level of mental, physical, psychological, spiritual, and sexual then you have a beautiful thing in your life that should bring you great love and joy.

There will come a time that you are able to share your deepest and darkest thoughts with this person and you will begin to understand why they fell in love with you, and you fell in love with them. There is a mutual respect, and you both have shared some of the greatest hurt and didn't even know it. To be able to open to someone and express your emotions and your feelings to them takes time and effort.

True intimacy is something that you will experience with someone who is genuine and ready and willing to love you. When you come across a man or a woman that can make love to you and touch your soul and your spirit at the same time it becomes an event in your life that you will never forget. This is the type of thing that she has always wanted in her life and to be with a man that was not afraid to love her completely was a dream come true to her.

This feeling is going to be like no other you have ever had. This person is going to come into your life like a train and blow your mind. This is what has happened to me. I met someone and we hit it off quickly. I didn't see things coming when I made the move to give it a shot. He was so sweet and kind, loving and caring but most of all he was very honest about his life and his past. No one has a perfect life and I know that firsthand, but it is truly refreshing to have someone feel so good about you that they can open up and tell you everything and anything to make you more comfortable with them.

How this all began, the day that he laid his eyes on her were the first moment of how he found a lady that he felt was going to change his life forever. When they met it was a clear night outside and the moon was shining. He walked up to the porch where she was standing and she looked at him and thought, wow.

This could be the best moment of her life. She seemed shy at first and he grabbed her and hugged her. That very moment that they held each other was a magic spark that started the love that would bring them to a new start in both of their lives. He looked into her eyes and said to her, I know that this is soon, but I have never felt like this before. When someone comes into your life and they are able to touch your soul without touching your body is a very real emotion on so many levels. This is not going to be easy for someone who has been hurt and mistreated in the past. Sometimes you have to sit back and allow that person to talk when they are ready to help you understand what they have been through and how they really feel inside. Sure you can jump out there and allow things to happen for the moment but in the end it will mean nothing because you didn't get to understand what was going on for you both.

He would walk with her and hold her hand and kiss her hand and tell her how much he appreciated her being in his life. That was the start of something magical. He would tell her how important she was to him and how happy she made him, and he didn't want to lose that feeling.

You have shown her a new start of what could give her a great new way to live her life. There was going to be a new way to view how a relationship was supposed to be and how things between two people who shared so much in common that lived from two different worlds. She was from a sheltered family, but the family was very big in comparison to most, and he was from a small family, but he lived his life in a very different way from what she was used to, and he had lived out in the world where she was never allowed to go in her life.

She didn't know about how people were from life past experiences, but she was willing to learn from him. What they shared from the start was special and real on both sides. They shared bad histories, they shared bad habits, and they shared bad things that most people would have never thought from either of them. What they brought to each other was a change of how to do things in a different way to make each other happy and feel a love that they had never seen in their life before. No Drama!!!

When most people come into your life, they will leave a footprint that may show you something that you have never seen before but with this new life change it was very different. He never dreamed that he would find someone who he could relate to in a way that he had never done in his life before now. What she showed him was a new way to express himself without the anger and frustration that he has seen in the past.

This was going to be something new for both since she has been through some tough situations in her past that left her feeling broken and alone. When they came together there seemed to be a newfound renew on how to interact with the opposite sex and enjoy it while they were doing it. He had been in a bad situation and was with someone who left him broken and distraught. He felt like no one could love him because of the things he had endured in the past. She tried to get him to understand that he was special in his own way and they he needed to stop being down on himself and learn to deal with things as they come and make the best of it until the right one came along to see his worth.

This was a fresh new world that had to take time to explore on both sides of the fence. When they spent time together it just seemed like it was just the two of them, she had people around her and he had people around him but at that moment when they were together it was always just the two of them. No one else ever came into the picture. He was able to talk to her and express himself in ways that he had never done before and this was all new to him.

No one else ever came into the plan of what was getting ready to form between their new lives. This was going to be an explosion that neither of them could have imagined seeing in this lifetime. He was so special and unique in many ways different from what she was used to dealing with in relationships. He was a true gentleman. He did things for her that she had never experienced in her life, and she didn't know how to just sit back and accept it at first. He told her that he wanted to be her partner, her best friend, her lover and try going a different route from the past. It all sounded great, but she had to learn how to do these things because in her past she was always doing everything for everyone. No one ever took the time to do anything for her and show her that she was important too.

What was going to happen here was a challenge of how to interact with a man/woman and never see anyone or anything but that person. She got to see how love can grow for someone that you just met because you had to take the time to sit and talk to that person and learn about them.

What they liked or didn't like. How to talk to them in a way that was going to reach a part of them that had never been touched before. When you find someone that you can connect with on a level of comfort and stability then you are sure to have the intimacy that you have never had in your life.

They were the difference of night and day, the stars and the moon, the heart, and the soul. This is going to be a very time-consuming event in the lives of both. This is going to create a big change for both to figure out how they are going to control the feelings that they have never felt before and to control them with someone that they just met and fell head over heels for.

It is safe to say that the feelings will take control of the emotions and show them both that they have no say in the matter of the heart. It is going to be strong, hard, and come from out of know where. It is going to hit them like a ton of bricks, and they will never see it coming.

She was once a lady who fell hard for a guy and jumped too fast, and he was a guy who fell for the girl who told him that she loved him, and he never knew why? It was a mystery to both, but this was a journey that was different and new on both sides. On both sides of the fence there can be challenges and despair but in the end you have to know how to take things in stride and keep moving in order to get to where you are trying to go.

This is going to be a love story that will unfold to give people a new outlook on what love is truly about and how it is meant to start, grow, and end up. She never dreamed that she could be this happy, but God proved her wrong. In her eyes, she was not worthy of good man, she was used to dealing with dead beats and no-nonsense men who just didn't care about life or what it really had to offer.

Most of her life she had been used and allowed it to happen because she was down on herself. She always had big dreams but never really knew how to achieve them till she met this man. Her heart was fully open for the first time in her life that she could feel the way that she felt and knew that she had real love in her life.

When they looked into each other's eyes there was no one there but them. They spent a lot of time talking getting to know all that they could about each other. There was much to understand as to why two people who had been through so much hurt and pain could find an instant love. She says that it was the fate of God, he soon agreed. This is going to be a lesson learned about how to deal with people and learn how to understand what you are getting ready to go through.

Together they would start a beautiful love that could be seen by everyone and anyone who saw them together. People said to them on many occasions that you guys must have a long loving marriage to be so happy. But the funny response was always we are not married yet, this is just the beginning for us.

We are growing an outstanding relationship not only with each other but with God as the foundation to how happy we become. Now it is funny how she looks at him and sees so much love and joy and he look at her and he sees a woman he never dreamed he would have in his life.

Before they came together, they both spent time surfing dating sites and trying to see if they could find what they both felt that they were missing. She looked in all directions and under rocks and turned over a few dangerous bugs that could have been fatal. But in the end God took her out of those situations and made her be still. She had to understand that if she was trying to drive her life nothing would work for her.

When they met, this was going to be a special adjustment to be seen. It takes time to feel a person out and get the feelings of what you are going to experience will keep you going. You are going to see things and hear things that are going to be new and a trial and error type of theory that is going to help you to see what this person is all about.

He on the other hand was pouring himself into trying all that he could to make his relationships work but at the same time he was leaning away from God in his life, and he was doomed to be unhappy until he came to see that he was lost.

They both have had the same thoughts that why their lives were plagued with so much heart ache and pain and not more joy and happiness. She spent time with herself looking into her heart as to what she was doing wrong and she kept coming up with the same answer, she didn't allow God to be the driver.

She had to understand that life was rough because when you choose to go after things yourself without the love of God to guide you then it will never work out. He showed her that she was worth way more than she thought. He gave her a new look on life, she felt secure and appreciated for the first time in her life and it was all due to his love for her. She needed to find a way to love herself more than anything and anyone. When you are able to open your eyes and your heart to someone who God has chosen for you then you will find a magical thing in your life that is unsurpassed and can't be broken.

Now we have a new way of life for to see how things could be great if they allowed the higher power to lead the way. Most people won't want to accept that there is a higher power, but they believe and that is what matters to them right now. If they can work together, love hard and work hard accomplish the things in life that they both agree on then they are on the right road to being happy.

Over the course of time between these two people things start to happen and it takes them both by surprise. He would look at her with shock when she tells him that she has started to have real feelings for him, he is not used to having a woman of her high standards tell him that she wants to be with him and not want anything from him but his love.

He is used to seeing woman who have that give me attitude that have no interest in getting anything out of life except a handout from others.

This is all new territory for him, and he is trying to figure out a way to grasp what is taking place in his life with this new woman coming along when she did. He had been hurt, abused, and mistreated by women in the past. This may sound funny to some but yes men go through this too. It is harder for them to deal with the reality in front of them when a woman mistreats them because the first thing that they do is blame themselves for everything going wrong.

Sometimes we as woman need to take responsibility for what we do wrong and fix it. Intimacy is no about sex. We are talking about something that is hard to find and even harder to keep. This is when two people can come together and enjoy each other without saying a word.

Just the feeling and the touch of each other says it all and if you ever find this type of connection with someone, I say that it is a rare find. Keep it close to you and never allow anyone to get in the middle of creating a love that you may never find again.

She is one who can admit that she failed in relationships in the past. Giving too much, not expecting more, not taking the upper hand to acknowledge that she deserved more out of life than just sex. Yes, this is the issue here, when you allow yourself to be mistreated by another person and it boils down to all you have together is sex, then you must look at yourself to see where you went wrong.

Now the tell all story here is that when a man and a woman come together will there be sparks off the back or will it take time to build on something that can be real down the road. Well, when they met, it was a shock to both that the stars had aligned and came to them as a sign that this was going to be a good thing. They spent a lot of time talking, getting to know all about each other, sharing secrets, past pain, hurt, good things and bad.

On both end of the coin, you will see that there will come a time in everyone's life that you will come across someone who will either change your life or destroy it. It is really a contest to see which will strike first.

I think that this lady has seen a new spark for the first time in her life and all the past relationships that she has been involved in allowing herself to be used to get satisfaction and then this man comes along and doesn't want anything from her but her heart. He seemed too good to be true in the beginning and she had to take a step back to make sure she wasn't going to fast and seeing things that really weren't there.

When they come together and spent quality time with each other it is always magic. They could sit on the porch for hours and just look at each other without saying as much as a word. They could see into each other's souls, and they had so much fun talking and learning about each other.

Now it took more than they both expected to take that first step to see if this was, they both wanted to do. Getting into a new relationship when you hear so many horror stories about how people meet and get together and then they either don't work out, one of them goes crazy on the other one, something happens to where there is violence that comes into play, or it just was not meant to happen in the first place.

When you meet someone new and they bring a joy into your life that you can't explain, you will then sit down and try to understand that what you are now dealing with is from a higher power.

The day came about, and she was feeling some type of way. Her emotions were all over the place and She finally broke to the degree that she jumped the gun and took it out on her man, and he flipped. She had a breakdown and was not sure how to handle her feelings. She wanted to talk to him and explain to him what was on her mind. He left upset and she knew that she was in a bad place.

There were so many things going through her mind when he left, and she knew that at that point she may not see him again. He had become her best friend, her knight in shining jeans. She had a pain in her stomach that was taking her breath away. She felt sick and couldn't fix it.

She has come to a place where she was alone again and was not sure what to do next. She was scared and needed him more now than ever, but she ran him away because she was dealing with some emotions that she couldn't control. She enjoys when he comes around and he really loves it when she gets his attention and his affection, but this was a bad day and for her there was no way to go back.

She must now deal with the fact that he had feelings for her, and she had feelings for him, but her past was getting in the way. They both have been through so much and finally found someone who could understand that they both were hurting but she messed up.

Days fall into nights, and she is sleeping alone wishing he was there with her to hold her. She needs him so bad, but she is not in a place to ask him for anything else after today. She feels that her time with him is over and now she must make peace with that mistake. She fell in love with him and maybe it was too soon for her to let her feelings out there to him, but she did one night after making love to him. She felt so close to him. She felt like she had found the one person who truly understood her problems, past and the bigger goal for them to work together and build a great life.

This is not the place that she wanted to be. Things were going well, and she was finally feeling like there was someone who cared about her and was maybe falling in love with her for the good-hearted person that she was. It is so hard to explain because she is fighting back the tears to make the notes that she is trying to get down on paper. If the time is now, then she sees the end of what could have been a great thing in her life.

This was going to be a very special day or them. He keeps reminding her that she is so special to him, and he appreciated her being in his life. She is keeping him grounded and keeping him together. It seems that she is getting closer to him more and more every day. They have a very close-knit bond that they didn't see coming.

This is a friendship that is blooming into more than friends and they both felt the connection to each other. She loved to be around him and his energy, he loved to talk to her because she listened to what he had to say. They could converse and bounce things off each other and they laugh about the outcome of the solution.

The love that they have shared over the past few months had shown them both that they could find love and be happy because it does exist. She had been abused in the past and he had been mistreated. Many people don't understand that men can be abused by women just like women can be abused by men. They both had so much pain to recover from but the time that they spent together seemed to remove a lot of what they had been though.

He never wanted to hurt her, he wants to love her and show her how much a woman should be appreciated by the man that loves her. She believed he was falling in love with her and when he told her she fell apart inside. She had come to the point in her life that she was going to be alone because most men that she met just wanted to play games and she was way too mature to get into another situation that caused her any more grief. She was giving up on finding love.

The day that they met was amazing to them. If you had to go back to a special moment in your life, then this would be it. He can sit for hours and look into her eyes and see the love growing in her heart. She is a very special lady to him; he shows her daily how much she means to him, and she gives the same back to him. They are a great couple but not official yet. They complement each other in so many ways. He loves being close to her because she throws off a positive energy and he loves how it feels in his life. He has learned to look at things in a different way because of how she makes him feel.

When you come across someone in life that you had never planned on meeting it is called a chance encounter. This is what this was. There was no way that they would have thought that the day that they laid eyes on each other it would change their lives forever. She was in a shell, sad, scared, and self-conscious about herself. He was strong, secure, and savvy about living his life to the fullest. These were qualities that they could pass on to one another and get the benefits of both sides of the coin. He never felt like this about a woman in his life and she knew that she was very special to him at that time with the things that were going on between them.

They would spend hours together. Talking, going over the past and thinking about all the things that got them to this point in the place of love where they were.

He always made her feel some type of way bout him when her was close to her. He was a very special man. He was a good guy who had been dragged through some things in his life just like she had and together they were always able to understand the issues that the other person had at that time.

She had to learn about the true facts of learning how to love someone who is willing to be in her life for the right reasons and wanting to unconditionally love her the way that she always dreamed of at this point in her life.

When you meet someone, and they are really wanting to be in your life you must get out of your own way. This means that you have to stop doing what you did in the past and allow yourself to enjoy the new love from someone who is there in your life trying to be loved just like you are.

Being able to allow yourself to get close to someone is hard enough without feeling like you are under pressure to do anything that you are not ready for. When you start a new relationship, you must allow yourself to grow with that person and learn to be close to them on all levels. You can't just jump out there and act like you have known them all your life and just do things out of the normal. IT takes time to grow and share things that you both can enjoy and adapt to. This is called the stage of learning and growth.

Intimacy is a rare gift. This is something that you are going to share with someone that has come into your life on a level that you never imagined. Intimacy is not sex. It is a bond that you build with someone that you are trying to get close to. This is where you spend time with a person, create memories of happy times that you share and enjoy the connection that you both have when you are together and not.

This is going to be a big deal when you meet someone because you are not looking for sex, you are searching for a love that you have never had before. There comes a time when you know that there is more to life than just jumping into bed with someone that has no meaning to your life. Either to enhance it or come to cause you pain and heartache. Intimacy is a gift that two people will share and create something special that is not just for one of you but for the both of you to enjoy. I truly believe that the entire point to being intimate is having fun together. This part of your relationship is built on trust, love, companionship for one another and the honesty that you provide in a total package. Without these main four ingredients your time together is going to be very short lived.

When a man and woman come together and find that they have a mutual connection of other things in their lives that can bring them closer together, this is going to be an adventure for good loving. Being able to talk to that person on any level, hold a meaningful conversation and be able to adapt to the surroundings and atmosphere around them is going to be a great start to what will be a great relationship only because you both are investing in something special. I keep expressing this term Intimacy because this is a very special tool that most people take for granted. When you create a bond with someone special, you are going to understand what it really means to have this type of love for someone and know that they have your best interests at heart in the end. There is never going to be a time that you meet someone and fall instantly in love with them and just go all out for them.

There is a time and place for everything that is going to happen in your life and the best part of you new relationship is going to be how good it feels when you are sharing your love with this person and how intimate you get with them in the end. Coming together in a way that you have never shared with someone is a feeling like no other. Being able to not only touch them physically but mentally and emotionally will have you going through things in your mind that you never imagined. These are feelings that will make you rethink your past relationships because you are seeing things in a different light.

This is a connection with someone who you are giving your soul too. Sometimes you will embrace a feeling that you think is real, but it is a physical feeling that is not going to bring you anything but pain because it is not the person that you should be with at that time in your life.

The Fun—Stage 3

. . . .

This is the time of your relationship that you are supposed to get close to each other and enjoy each other company when you can do so and you can find things to do that you both enjoy and have fun together. I have always enjoyed bowling, so this is always a ice breaker for me when I meet someone. Let's go bowling and see what you got...

They were both acting like teenagers who had met someone new for the first time and fell deep in love with them and had no idea as to what was going to happen next to them that would change their lives forever.

One day you wake up and find yourself in a situation that you never imagined you would be in You fell in love and then the love faded. You had a guy in your life, and you thought at that time that you guys were going to be together forever.

Now the day comes that you are confused and angry as to why he won't touch you or love on you or make love to you!!! It is a hurtful feeling to have someone in your life that you have no connection too.

The reality that you are thinking it is something wrong with you and then you go onto a deep depression of what have you done wrong? What did you not give enough of? The result is that it is not you. You gave all that you could give but some people are not able to love anyone because they don't love themselves. At the end of the day the best result here is to find your own happiness and move on.

Now with all the drama that has been going on and you are feeling down on yourself, you can't see what is coming right at you. The door will open, and you will see a new beginning. If you have never seen this before then you are going to be in for a big surprise. When you allow time to feel the love of yourself then you can allow yourself to enjoy the love of someone else.

Here you wake up one day with a new outlook on life. You are looking to find some joy in your life so that you can smile again and show everyone around you that you are moving on. You have been in a place of darkness for a long time and now the sun will shine. In the next days ahead, you are going to see that you have been missing out on so much time and attention from the man that you had already given your life too. You wake up on this day and see a new light in your eyes.

Here you are out and about, and you run into this guy who is new to the area. He is a hard-working man; he enjoys spending time with family and he enjoys some of the same things that you do. You guys sit down and start a conversation. If you were a gambling woman you would never have seen this coming. This is going to be a very special day for the both of you. When you get a chance to sit down and talk it seems like you have known each other for many years.

Here is a place of excitement. Pure joy of being with someone who can understand you and see where you are coming from and the things that you enjoy doing makes him smile because they are simple things that you can do together. If you enjoy creating things, then he does too. If they have a mutual love for poetry and writing, then that brought them closer together because they shared ideas and bounced things off each other.

There is an instant chemistry between you. You are noticing that you are both laughing so hard, and you are trying to understand what is going on right now. This is a very strange feeling for the both of you because you have been through some hurtful things, and you are trying to comprehend what is going on that is so different from before.

This day starts off as every other day had since you met him a few weeks prior. You are going to let your guard down and allow him to show you something that you have been missing.

When you finally come around to get the idea that this man is not going to hurt you or play with you then you really allow yourself to open to him and express your feelings. Little do you know that he is feeling some of the same things that you are feeling. This is strange for you because you are not used to a man telling you how he feels.

You guys plan a date, this is going to be special, Dinner, movie, and fun. You can't remember how long it has been that you have done anything like this in the past, but he reminds you to not think about the past, let's focus on the future and only that. Tonight, is going to make you see a new dawn coming. This is going to be a night that you both will never forget.

You meet for dinner; this is special because you guys get to sit down and not only enjoy each other's company, but you can explore some new things. He opens the car door, he pulls out your chair, he tells you that you are beautiful and that is something that you have not heard in a very long time. He is scoring extra points and you think he knows that. He is making you feel special, and all the attention is making your mind go crazy.

You are not sure what to say or do at this point. You don't want to tell him too much because you don't want to run him off, but you don't want to not say enough because he may think that he is not doing enough to see that smile on your face. He says to you that he is happy that you are there with him and you tell him that you have been thinking about him all day. Now comes the dinner. You guys get to indulge on good food, conversation, and drinks.

The night is coming to an end, and he take you home. He kisses you goodnight and he tells you that he had an awesome time with you. You are blushing with joy. You are seeing stars. This is a moment in your life that you have waiting for and all the relationships you have been through didn't prepare you for anything like this to happen. This night is going down in the books as the best date ever. You had a man who enjoyed some quality time with you and dare to ask if you wanted more.

You guys plan the next meeting, this is going to take place in a park, he wants to make sure you are comfortable with being around him and he sees your smile from across the parking lot. You guys somehow manage to get together again and then decide to take a walk down the trails. This is something that neither one of you have done since you were both young.

You are walking and then next thing you notice is that the conversation is getting intense. Here you go again, this Is not something that you are used to doing. He then grabs your hand, and you are worried that he is going to make a move.

He pulls you close to him, and he says that he is having the time of his life. Your heart skips a beat. You are trying to figure out what is going on. As you both are enjoying the walking on the trails you seem to be passing other couples and they look at you guys as such cute people who are really enjoying each other.

Now you find a place to sit and talk. Once you sit down, he pulls you close to him and kisses you in the neck This is sending chills though your body, but you don't think he sees it just yet. This is a feeling that you have been waiting for and you are starting to like it. He tells you that he is going to spoil you. If the time ever felt right, it is right now with the both of you sitting in the park on a clear night enjoying each other and having fun.

You can't imagine what is going through his mind right now because you are so happy to be there with him you are about to burst. If you ever thought of the perfect moment with someone this must be it. You have never felt like this, and you are showing how much you really appreciate all that he has done in the short period of time since you guys met.

The time is passing, and you guys are enjoying each other's company so much that you don't realize the time has flown by and it is getting dark. The sun has set, and you feel the joy of being with a man who truly is giving you the attention that you have been craving for so long. At the end of the night together you guys share a passionate kiss, and you go on your way.

He tells you that he is going to call you when he gets in and gets settled for the night and he never disappoints you. This is a true feeling that you have never had in your past relationships, and you are feeling the love from all directions.

The next time that you guys meet up is a very special moment because this is something that you both have been planning all week long. This is the time that you are going to really see where things are going to go. You are going to allow yourself to let go and figure out what you have been missing in your life all this time.

He calls you early in the day, you guys are planning an evening meeting and the time and place are set. This is going to be intense because you have never done anything like this before and in the past, you always made the excuse that you couldn't get away from one reason or another.

For some reason this man is different and has you on some different road that you have never traveled before, but you are loving this feeling that he Is giving you, so you are going to roll with him on this night. The moon is glazing out of the clouds, and you are looking through the sunroof of his car and thinking what am I about to do?

No need to worry about he says, it is going to be alright. You don't have to worry or be scared because we are both grown, and we know what we what to do. We get to the spot, we got a room for the night, it is going to be so special until you get there, and things start taking off...

Now you are feeling this way because you are having feelings that you have been suppressing for many years and a man that wants to fulfill your every dream. You create a mood, you set up candles, you have a sexy outfit just for his eyes and he has a music play list that you both are enjoying.

The lights are dimmed down, he puts the music on, and you both are enjoying the conversation and then the moment hits you both that it is time to stop talking because the feelings are taking over your bodies and you want to be in his arms and do more than talk.

He starts off kissing you on your neck, this is making your body do things that you have never experienced before. He lays her on the bed, and he starts to caress her body, now she is getting feelings like she is in shock. He is running his strong hands all over her body and she is trying to hold back the temptation that she is feeling at that moment.

When he makes love to her, he takes her breath away and holds her in his arms and just caresses her hair and loves on her till they fall asleep. She loves the way that he handles her body. He is not afraid to touch her and play with her and make her smile. He does whatever he needs to do to keep her smiling because in the beginning when they first met, he told her that he would make it his mission to see her smile every day and never feel sad or lonely again.

When you have a man touch you in a way that you have never had done before it will do something to your body, and you are not going to be in control of what happens. You lay there and allow him to have his way with you and before you know it that time has passed over and you are now making love to this man and giving him your entire being.

He is making you feel like a woman should feel. He is giving you the pleasure that you forgot about. He is making you see things that you had never dreamed of, and you are doing things with him that you never thought you would do with anyone. He is not only touching your body, but he is touching your soul. He is taking away all the pain that you have been dealing with and making you forget about all your troubles.

The day will start off on a sunny morning and they both awaken after laying in each other's arms all night getting to know one another and talking. This was a very special moment for both since neither of them had ever done anything like this before.

He could touch her and make her go wild. He would rub her hair, play with her body, and drive her crazy. She had never felt like this before in any or her relationships and she made sure to let him know just how he made her feel all the time that they were together.

He runs his hands down her legs and thighs. He touches her stomach and tells her how much he is really feeling her at that moment. He sees her as a beautiful woman, and he is going to enjoy all of her. He reached a spot where she moans, and he is getting excited about how she is letting go and feeling with him. She was able to relax and lay back and feel things that she had missed out on with other men. She was never going to forget this night because there were a lot of firsts going on. There were sparks in that room that lit up the night's skies. He was making love to this woman, and she was losing control.

Afterwards, they laid there together, and she laid on his chest and he held her and rubbed her hair and they fell asleep in each other's arms. The next morning was amazing too. They got up, took a shower together and then they made love again. He was truly giving her what she had never had in the past.

He was not afraid to love on her and make her feel good. He loved to see her smile. That was his gift from her. She could smile and light up any room that they were in. He could find her in a crowd because he knew that smile over everything. Her smile is what caught his attention in the first place. She never had a man tell her how special she was, never had anyone really treat her like this and show her so much attention and affection for no reason.

The best thing about the night is that when it is all over you lay on his chest and you guys talk the night away. It was something that you both needed and that you both were so excited to experience together. She would fall asleep in his arms, and you feel like a new woman. This is the new start that you have been craving in your life for a very long time. How is it that this man knew just what you needed it and he gave it to you.? The next morning you guys wake up together and you are trying to figure out what took place the night before. You are smiling from ear to ear, and he is smiling which it was something that he rarely did before meeting you.

You both had been through some bad situations and needed to have a moment of just letting go. He came along when you were at the low point in your life, and he knew just what to do to bring you out of the mess in your mind that was consuming you.

Now the date is over, and you must go back to the place that you needed to get away from for a few hours. You are in a different place right now. You are filled with so much joy and feeling like a different woman. You have a pep in your step that has never been there and for those who know you will be able to see that you are different.

There is no better feeling than that of a man who has given a woman pure joy and ecstasy even if it was a short time that you had with him, it was all worth it for that moment of peace of mind that she needed.

She would never be the same after that night that she spent with him. He treated her like a woman, he gave her conversation, intimacy and then rocked her world. This part is funny because when you are searching for something that is missing in your life and you come across it like that you are never the same again.

He gave her some things that she had only heard about when talking to her girlfriends. He treated her the way a man should treat the woman that he claims to care about. This gave her a new outlook on her next move and what she needed to do next in her life to get things moving in the right direction for herself. If she ever had any doubts before they are all gone thanks to this man that had come into her life and changed the game.

He had been dealing with some major issues in his life and he came to her for support. That is the one thing that he always knew she could give him, and he loved her for that. He gave his heart to her and allowed himself to be free to tell her anything. He broke down and gave in to his feelings of what he was feeling about her being in his life and how much she meant to him. She changed him in ways that he never thought were possible.

When he talked about her to people, he had a glow in his eyes and people knew that this was the one that he had to hold on too. She gave him stability in ways he didn't know were possible and how she always knew what he needed when he needed it was just amazing to him. She could read his heart not his mind, she was able to look into his eyes and see a part of him that he didn't see himself.

This was a woman on a mission to not only find love but to be loved by a man that truly wanted to love her back in ways that she had never experienced in her life. Once she was able to let go and give herself completely to him and allow him to take her places, she always wanted to go then together they could explore their needs and wants together and grow from that as time went on.

He was so different from any other. He was compassionate with her; he loved on her body and caressed all her curves. He touched her in ways he hadn't done before, there was something different this time around. He was emotional with her, yet he was firm and giving her the stability that she was looking for.

They have shared some very hurting feelings about things that they have been through in their past relationships and really don't want to get into the same mistakes that caused them pain but trying to find some new ways to love and see if happiness is in the cards for them to explore together as a couple and starting a new life as one. She had finally found in a man the love and respect that she had searched for all her life. No one wants to get into a relationship and get hurt.

There have been days that they are together all the time and neither one of them seems to complain about that. They have both missed out on so much needed love and they found it in each other. This is a special attraction for them both because neither one of them have ever experienced love like this in their past relationships.

He lived his life in the fast lane and came up from a background of the streets. She was raised in a conventional home and wasn't aware of what the streets could do to your life till she fell on a part of her life that was hurtful and hard to survive but she did, and it made her a stronger woman because now she was more around to see what was coming at her and how to handle it.

He found something in her that she didn't know was there until she met him. There were parts of her life that she felt like she was just making it to survive because no one understood her hurt and pain. This man came along at the right time and swept her off her feet in the sense that he was showing her things that she had never experienced before in any of her past relationships. He was not afraid or scared to love her the way he knew she needed to be loved by a real man.

If you have ever had a man in your life that took your breath away when he touches you or made you feel so special that you didn't understand how or why he did it, trust me this is a feeling of love. He came into her life when she was at a low point of feeling unwanted. She was hurting and trying to figure out her next step, but she was stuck in a place of darkness that she was scared and unsure of her feelings and what she needed to do to get out of this funky place. What she was now going through was so confusing to her because she was always used to overseeing things in her relationships, but this man was very different. She was going down a path that she had prayed for and asked God to show her a new way of life so that she could find some happiness. Her smile was very contagious, and he made a vow to her to make her smile every day that they were together. He was a rare guy; he knew how to treat her to make her feel special because he always told her that she was a very special part of his life and he never wanted to be without her. He would be lost without her because she had given him some peace in his life that he had never seen or experienced with any other woman.

Not only was he touching her mind, body, and soul, she was touching him in ways he had never felt before. She was able to get into his mind and ease him when he was dealing with things mentality that had never been done for him in his past relationships.

He was undergoing a new experience in his life and to some it might scare then but for him he was embracing the adventure of this woman showing him a love he never knew before.

To have fun with someone with no holds barred back from you both getting to enjoy each other on a level that no one has ever seen from you and then to enjoy it as you are creating memories together is priceless. Love is a magical thing when used the right way. There is no such thing as too much love but there is however a thing called not enough love for anyone. I truly believe that when you meet someone there is a such thing as love at first site to the opposite sex, but it will all depend on what you both are looking for when you meet. I know that for me I have had many first loves but one a few have captivated me enough to say that I found and lost my true love.

When you have someone that you can laugh with. You spend time together learning about each other and figuring out the little things that make each other happy and sad. If you want to have fun, then you must put yourself out there to show the side of you that most people don't get to see. You are Humble, you are kind, you are funny, but you don't see this often because of the way you hold back your heart and keep things bottled up. This is the part of your relationship that you find things to do together as a couple. This is going to be where you guys find time for each other when you thought you didn't have the time to do anything. Here is when you make each other laugh, love, and feel wanted and needed because you have found a love in someone that makes you smile and feel like a kid again.

The Reality Versus the Dream—Stage 4

If you are falling in love with the person in your life, then you have to be able to understand the difference between the reality and the dream of what you are experiencing. Love is very hard but it gets even harder when you lose someone that you really care about because of a silly mistake.

When you come across a man or a woman in your lifetime that you have been searching for the reality will hit you that they had to go through some things to get to where they were in their life and then when you guys meet up it will be become an event in the lives of both of you that will change you in ways that you could have not thought or dreamed of coming.

So now we have a situation where two people have come together to create a new love and the joy of watching that love grow is going to be amazing... If you have ever seen a man or woman, feel so low in their life and to meet someone that just helped to allow them to show who they really are will give you a new outlook of love and life. Sometimes the thought of spending your life alone is ok for some people but not everyone. We have learned to enjoy the company of a companion and learn to share things with that person that you don't just share with anyone.

It has been a long hard time for people to understand in this world that the difference between love and being in love is rare. This is going to be an eye-opening experience and when it happens to you, then you will understand what this section was all about.

Joy and happiness are all about what you make of it. No one will be able to live life in misery and despair for long. You must find some joy at some point. When you find love, don't run from it. Allow the time that it will take to see it grow and watch how things can turn your life into a place that you would have never imagined. This story is about finding love, being in love and the real meaning of what love can do for two people who are missing out of the joys of giving love to another person and receiving love back.

In the first stage of what they were doing was getting to know each other on levels that neither of them had touched before. She was an introvert, kept to herself didn't have many friends because others couldn't understand her and what she was going through. Females would say that she was crazy for letting herself go like she did and allowing this man to take her places she had never been. You just don't do stuff like that with anyone. You really must know the man first before you just let go like that. This is not real, when you meet people, you never know if they are going to be good or bad for you, that is called taking a chance to see what will happen. But she knew that he was the one to do it with having been with him for a few months, she gave herself of heart, mind, body, and soul. He was able to touch her in ways she had never been touched and a real woman just wants a man to appreciate her in every way and only want her.

This man didn't come at her with the lame talk like most men had done in the past. He came to her honest, open, and allowed her to make the choice is she wanted to keep it moving forward. He was honest with her about his past and gave her the option if she felt like he was worth the chance. They have both been through so much and to finally have someone real was a great challenge to her because she didn't know how to take him at first site. The reality here is that people come in all ways into your life for a reason or a season. We must learn how to weed them out without losing what could be a good thing for us. If you have the time to sit and talk to someone then you can find out if you have things in common with that person then I say give it a chance to see if something can grow.

Here were at stage two, they are seeing each other every day, he calls her to just check in and say that he is thinking about her. She is having the time of her life because she is getting love and attention from a man who wants to be a part of her life and make her happy. He touches her body and makes her quiver with emotions; he can touch her hand when they are sitting in the car just talking and it makes her feel some type of way toward Him. They met in the strangest way, and he feels like she is the angel that was sent to him to help him find his way to greatness. He has a magnetic field around him that is keeping him going and she must find a way to get through it to find the real him. They both have seen and been involved in bad relations but they both had the same goal. Find real love.

He had so many thoughts running around his mind, and she was able to help him get them to make things happen. He trusted her with his life and his heart. He never asked her for anything but somehow, she knew when he needed things and just got them for him. When he looked around, he had just what he needed, and he had her too. This wasn't the typical lady he had been with in his life because she knew him in ways that he never dreamed anyone could or would know him.

What they shared is so powerful that is scares them both at times. He tells her that she means the world to him, and she shows him how much he means to her. If the world was not round, then he would driving a straight line all the time. She cares for him because at the end of the day he is giving her what she had been missing most of her life. Real love and real attention. He was an Alpha male, strong, independent, and able to maintain a family all by himself because most of his life just like her he was in relationships but was alone. This was going to be tough because she was an Alfa female due to living her life taking care of everyone around her in all situations. She had to learn to allow this man to lead her and guide them into a new dynamic and he had to understand that he had someone who was strong and independent that could handle things just like he could. He had to understand that she was not the normal lady he was used to dealing with in his life and that he was not the basic man she had ever dealt with in her life. He was a real man who knew how to take charge and take care of his home. They came together and never dreamed that life would be so happy and full of great new experiences as they prepared to take this trip together. He showed her that she could be loved the right way since she had never experienced that in her past. Sometimes it is not how you do things but the way that you do things that leave an imprint in someone's life.

What they both were setting their sights on was about to come to them full throttle and when it hits them it will be the greatest gift in the world to both to experience it together. When they sat down and started talking about the life that they wanted, he realized that she was different, and she saw that he was real. When he told her something, he followed through with it and stayed true to his word.

Stage three because more complex because now we are dealing with the feelings of a man and a woman who have fallen deep in love and are trying to figure out what to do next with these feelings. After a night of making love and sharing some very intimate things with her, he seemed to get a big relief off his back, and he started to smile again. She enjoyed knowing that she could make him smile and they have fun together.

During the time of them being together she has seen different parts of him, and she knows that everyone has been through pain in their life but at that moment she saw so much pain in his eyes that she couldn't bear to see him going through this all alone. She laid in his arms and allowed him to break down and show is sensitive side that he never showed anyone. There would be times that they would cry together and find something more powerful than just love. He gave his heart to her and she kept it under her umbrella of loving him.

She was so very special to him, and he made sure that she knew that in that very moment. He had been dealing with some extra hardships in his life that were a big challenge to him but with her by his side he was going through it like a champion winning the battles that were set in front of him to see him fail. She would hold him when he cried, and they would cry together in each other's arms, but he never felt alone when he was with her because he had someone that truly was showing him what real love was all about.

This is an opportunity for both to see what the other person could bring to the table and find out if this was going to be a good fit for both to explore and enjoy a new and exciting life together. When he looked into her eyes, he saw nothing but love and joy. When she was sad, he knew how to cheer her up with just a word. He captivated her heart in a way that no other man could do. He was real. He was sincere and he was not out for a good time, he was looking for real love just like she was. They seemed to have found it witnessing a great new friendship blossoming into a love that they both have always dreamed of.

When he is close to her, he makes her feel like a queen. She is being cherished in a way that she has never experienced before. He makes her think about all the times that she was alone and looking for love and now she has it right in front of her eyes. He would look into her eyes and see her soul. He found a link to her heart that most men never got close to seeing because they mistreated her and she walked away. He touches her very softly because he wants to make sure that she knows that he loves her and appreciates her.

She is so overwhelmed by this new life that is in front of her that sometimes she thinks she is crazy. How could someone come from out of nowhere and fall in love with her and cherish her the way that he did. He had gone through a lot of pain in his life and contrary to what people believe men are being mistreated in relationships just like women are.

Communities in a large area can stop some of the violence against young women if they would get more involved with programs that will help to educate young girls on the real meaning of true love and what to look for and not to rush into anything just for the sake of saying that they have someone in their lives. This cannot be a process for just the parents; everyone has to get involved in trying to stop violence before it starts.

People also can encourage the media to generate nationwide coverage that will educate more Americans both men and women about sexual assault, dating issues and domestic violence, of women and men and the stalking; encourages people to take action to prevent more violence against women; and rallies support for local service providers.

Educating the media will help with these complex issues surrounding sexual assault, dating and domestic violence, and stalking. This in time will result in better news stories that will bring to the for front more attention about people that can make them aware of what is going on and help people to learn that the best issue of violence is not going to go away unless we come forward and stop what is going on.

Because when we spend the time to educate the media and the journalists about what is going on then we will cover the issues more comprehensively and effectively. This will also help the women to feel more comfortable about coming out to talk about what has happened to them and help them to deal with the issues that will take those months, sometime years to get over. This is going to open the doors for more people to come out and get the help that they need instead of turning to death and suicide.

America has generated stories for television stations and newspapers and in mainstream newspapers about marches against domestic violence in their neighborhood, but they never follow up on how they start when it comes to young women. Speeches and special group gatherings by survivors who live at a batterer's home will try to come forward until they are pushed into a corner or until they are scared to the point where they forget what really has happened to them.

At this point the abuser is going to get violent and cause more trouble to the person that they are abusing. More people now see the sexual assault of most women but it is still listed as a taboo for most that don't understand what it is and why it is going on in our country that is supposed to be the land of the free. Some states generated newspaper stories because of its unique public awareness campaign targeting girls between ages 14 and 16. This is something that should scare more parents to keep their kids closer or teach them that you can't be kind to everyone. Make sure that when you choose to get out of the bad situation that you are sure that you are not going to go back due to being sweet talked and that you are not going to change your mind after the fact. These are but a few ideas of successful strategies used by advocates to increase attention to violence against women.

Make sure that the final call is your call and that no one is going to change your mind once it is set to get out. No one can make this decision for you; it has to be everything that you know is right, and it has to be what you really want.

Educate the public about violence against women and find advocates who can partner with programs in the community that already target teens. Many organizations already work with teens on issues such as AIDS and HIV prevention, substance abuse prevention, violence prevention, conflict resolution, and sexuality education need to be just as important to our young people. Where effective programs exist, advocates should partner with these organizations to add information about sexual assault, dating and domestic violence, and stalking.

School-based projects serve to train the next generation of college leaders on the issues of sexual assault, dating and domestic violence, and stalking. These programs will be even more effective when the incoming college students who lead these programs have already been taught about issues related to violence against women.

I have found that more information goes out over the local radio and television stations before it actually hits the newspapers, and with this in mind we as a nation also react to negative information about the affects to our youth and young teens and with more and more information available anyone can get help if they want it and ask for it.

There is no shame in telling someone that you are being abused, the shame is keeping it too yourself and not doing anything about it. When you feel that you are all alone, then you need to find some solace in being able to award someone for a winning idea that will create a campaign that will offer help and assistance should and this can be an incentive to get more people in the public involved.

Partnering with the media can be important when planning for public service activities. If you are able to stay on a firm ground with the media then they can be used to get your point across and make sure that more people are aware of what is going on around them.

Many good examples of successful campaigns to help teens get through the tough pain of being an abused person, with the outline for the African-American community, there should be an open door policy for anyone who is being abused to get help. We need to find more projects to help promote self-esteem for all of our young people and prevent violence against our younger men and women.

We need to show our young people that it is not ok to be abused or to abuse something that you claim to love. Many programs try to encourage the young people to come out and get involved in the community so that they can see what is going on. But there are a lot of kids that have seen the abuse first hand, or have had to deal with it and that will make them scared to talk about it to others.

Many types of creative peer counseling groups and some of the most effective public education campaigns, which are becoming more wide spread have been able to show our youth that it is a nationwide problem and that we need to look at it to stop it from carrying on to our next generation. More high schools are getting involved with the on-site of keeping up with the children and now more than before we can depend on the college campuses to be more involved in what is going on there as well. It seems that today we have a wide spread need to be abused, or to abuse someone that we claim to love and if you have to do that then you need to learn what love is all about. Women who have been victims of violent crimes can benefit tremendously when television stations and networks, radio stations, newspapers, magazines, Web sites, and other media promote the phone numbers of local, state, and national sexual assault and domestic violence hotlines.

Today, local, state, and national campaigns inform victims of sexual assault, dating and domestic violence, and stalking about available services, communicate that violence against women is wrong, and promote behavioral change among the general public and in specific communities. In my layout of this book, I have shared some of my own issues and laid out the back plan to what went wrong and what I did to correct the problem. I wanted to make sure that when I wrote another book, it would be something that people could read and appreciate the angle to why I did what I did.

This book is to be used as a tool to help abused women; men and children get help, and find their way back to a normal life. If you think that is not possible, I am here to tell you that it is and you can do whatever you put your mind too if you try hard enough and keep fighting for a good future.

When you get to a point in your life that you feel all hope is gone then gives your life to prayer and ask the Lord to guide you in the right direction. If you give up on him then there is nothing left for him to do? For all the women in the world who felt that they had to carry the burden all alone. I am here to tell you to keep your faith close and your family closer. Keep in mind that abuse comes in all shapes, sizes, colors and backgrounds. If someone tells you that they would never hit you always be aware that the ones that say it are the ones that do it.

Don't depend on anyone to give you self-joy, give it to yourself. Why do you feel that it is ok for you to abuse a woman? You have a sister at home, a mother, a friend and I am sure that you would not want them to be hurt or mistreated so why is it ok for you to do it to someone else?

I have not been able to put my hand on what you were thinking when you did it to me but I am sure that when the time came and you had to get your life on track that you had to reevaluate what you did and see if it was right or wrong.

What do you see for your life? Can you find peace within yourself so that you don't have to abuse others? My hope here is that I can reach one person for them to see that the old saying "The apple doesn't fall far from the tree" does not have to be true to everyone. I have seen the true meaning of happiness with the life that I have now.

I want other people to see that the joy for living will be whatever you choose to make it and I hope that you can find the joy of happiness within yourself. If you have the ability to find love, then why not treat it with the respect that I am sure that most of you have been taught in your young years. If for no other reason than to not whine up in jail or dead from beating a women that had family who wouldn't put up with that. I have seen so much anger and pain from families because of the lack of being honest and admitting that there are hidden problems within the family and try to get help before it become abuse.

I am not talking about this subject because I have nothing else better to do but because I feel that there are so many people either women or men who have gone through this in their life and need help and maybe don't know where to find it. I have spent the past year working on trying to get help for those people who don't know where to turn and I am now seeing more and more places coming out of the woodwork to provide help before something of this nature happens to you.

I am not dead, I am not disabled, I am not handicap or disfigured, but I can say that I am lucky. I can speak from experience on this subject. You will have the low days and the high days and then you will feel that you have hit rock bottom. The bottom for me was not being able to talk to people that I loved and that where close to me. Manifesting the fire in your soul is going to bring you back to the reality of living life to the fullest.

I had to keep myself closed off from the world because I was ashamed of what I had gone through. When a woman goes through physical abuse, she will keep herself away from people because she will always feel that it was her fault as I did going through the turmoil that I had to live through many years ago.

The main thing that you have to remember is there is know where to go but up after all of that. If you have hit the end of the road and you can look yourself in the mirror and say, "I am still alive" then you still have things to do here on earth. I can say that no matter where you have come from that if you are truly able to find love within yourself then you too can make it too where I am now.

I have written two poetry books about love, hate, joy, pain, sorrow, and the main thing in the book was living. After all I had to be thankful that I was still alive and well enough to start all over again. It was tough in the beginning because I had to rebuild everything that I had and find a new safe place to call home.

Your life will become a stepping-stone that you have to climb one step at a time. You can't jump over things to get to the top you have to crawl till you are able to walk again. You need to see that all things do come to those who wait and for those who have to find a way to live it too will come to you.

Now we are going to get into a subject that will affect most if not all of the women who go through this horrible event in their lives: the children, your family, your friends and those people who love you and you have lost sight of them within yourself.

I never realized how many people loved me till I went into an abusive relationship and after it was all over how many people came out to help me get back up on my feet. I never gave much thought to going to church only because it was not something that I could do during the marriage. I never gave much thought about talking to my friends about the problem for the fear of being called stupid and dumb.

She is so overwhelmed by this new life that is in front of her that sometimes she thinks she is crazy. How could someone come from out of nowhere and fall in love with her and cherish her the way that he did. He had gone through a lot of pain in his life and contrary to what people believe men are being mistreated in relationships just like women are.

Sometimes when you meet someone new in your life, they come in a wave. This means that you don't know the reason that they came into your life when they did but at the same time you must be on guard before allowing them to get to close to your heart. The reality is that sometimes people come into your life to hurt you because you seem like an easy person to take advantage of. Then you have others that come into your life because they see something special in you that they want to be a part of. Either way it goes with the reality of love of the dream of love, you must take things slow and watch for warning signs and things that could be good or bad and keep your eyes open at all costs.

You have spent your life working on a dream of what the ideal relationship is going to be for you. When you meet someone, you are going to give your all into that person and then you are going to try to achieve something that you have never had when you were with the past people in your life. Real Love. When you meet a person, you have ideas of what you want in your life. You have fantasies of what you will enjoy with that person, and you have thoughts of what you and that person can create together. I believe that when someone comes into your life It can change you as a person. The reality is that sometimes people come into our lives to help us be better people and sometimes they can destroy us.

There will be times that someone will come into your life and make you feel like a princess and then there are times that someone will come into your life and make you feel like an ass. Falling in love is not an easy task to let your guard down and allow someone to get so close to you that you lose yourself in them. I have done this many times thinking that it was a good thing but, in the end, find out that I was lied too, used, and mistreated.

The day will come that you have to start over and for some people it is better to start over and create a new life than to live the nightmare that you have been forced into and unable to be happy with. It has been the biggest achievement for me when I started to work on creating poems that made me feel good. I entered a poetry contest one day and I few months later I got the news that I had won a prize. That was the best thing at that point in my life for me to feel safe again.

Now we come to the stage in your life where your family and friends will step in and show you that life is worth living and that you can do it after all that you have been through. The main thing that you need to see and understand is that just because you have been abused by someone that you loved or thought you loved does not mean that the next person that comes along will do the same thing.

I didn't want people close to me to see how foolish I had become over trying to love someone. I put my heart into the marriage and the relationship but nothing I did seem to matter unless it was money, drugs, and sex. It may be hard for people to understand that when you are caught into a situation such as this you feel that there is no way out.

Well that is a lie.

I found the way out and I got help. Now for the solution to what is going on. First of all we need to create groups, programs, and events for the young women so that they can understand that it is a behavior and that it is not acceptable for someone to hit you, abuse you in any kind of way and that we are not going to put up with it. We have to learn how to fight back before more of our young women wind up in abusive relationships or even worse, dead!!!

Here we have a society that is only looking out for themselves and for those people, women who ask for help or try to let someone know that this is going on no one will listen to them. If we can't find a safe place to go then how are we supposed to change our lives?

The Final Test—Stage 5

. . . .

Stage 5 is the final test. Here is where the love really starts for the to both of you to see if this is going to be the final test of what they have been working on trying to build. The piece of the puzzle that has not been easy to come by but well worth the wait. This is the point to where things become real for both.

This was going to be a very special day for them. He keeps reminding her that she is so special to him, and he appreciated her being in his life. She is keeping him grounded and keeping him together. It seems that she is getting closer to him more and more every day. They have a very close-knit bond that they didn't see coming.

This is a friendship that is blooming into more than friends and they both felt the connection to each other. She loved to be around him and his energy, he loved to talk to her because she listened to what he had to say. They could communicate and bounce things off each other and they laugh about the outcome of the solution.

The love that they have shared over the past few months had shown them both that they could find love and be happy because it does exist. They both had so much pain to recover from but the time that they spent together seemed to remove a lot of what they had been though. He never wanted to hurt her, he wants to love her and show her how much a woman should be appreciated by the man that loves her. She believed he was falling in love with her and when he told her she fell apart inside. She had come to the point in her life that she was going to be alone because most men that she met just wanted to play games and she was way too mature to get into another situation that caused her any more grief.

He was so different from any other. He was compassionate with her; he loved on her body and caressed all her curves. He touched her in ways he hadn't done before, there was something different this time around. He was emotional with her. He catered to her needs and wants at that moment, and he made sure that she knew that she was his lady. This is a term that he used with her when they were together because he always made sure that she knows how important she is to him and his stability.

They have shared some very hurting feelings about things that they have been through in their past relationships and really don't want to get into the same mistakes that caused them pain but trying to find some new ways to love and see if happiness is in the cards for them to explore together as a couple and starting a new life as one. He had been in some tough situations in his life and was not sure if he would ever find someone to love him for him. He was going through the same thing that she was, but the difference was the sex. He was a man, and she was a woman. The crazy thing is that people can experience the same effect of a trauma and have the same outcome.

She was abused in the past, so was he. She was mistreated in relationships and so was he. She wanted to find love and be happy and he wanted the same thing. She was finding herself and learning to love herself more and he was in that same place of self-love. For both, this journey was a true experience that they both needed and wanted.

They came together at the perfect time in their lives due to the fact that both of them had been through so much heartache and pain, now it was time to have love and happiness to enjoy and enhance their well-being.

She had finally found in a man the love and respect that she had searched for all her life. No one wants to get into a relationship and get hurt. He would give anything to see her smile. He fell in love with her smile and her laughter. She gave him something that only she could give to him because what they shared was only between them as a couple.

She was trying to focus on her living her life alone and he came in and changed all of that. He made her love again and she fell in love with him. He gave her stability, joy, and most of all the one thing that was so important to her the love of a man. not just saying it but showing it and his actions were always in her favor.

He never allowed a day to go by that she didn't know that she was very important to him in some way, shape or form. He never let her question if she was good enough, he proved it to her daily. He loved her mind, her body, her soul, and the biggest thing that he really loved was her curves. He admired her body in ways that she was just shocked by. He never let her feel that she was nothing more than important to him.

He enjoyed talking to her whenever he was able to do so because what they shared was a mental love as well as an emotional and physical one.

This seems to be a better place for them at this point. They are both going through some tough situations, and they are both able to lean on each other in ways that they never would have dreamed of. He is learning to allow her to care for him in a way that he has been searching for and she is able to let go of her demanding nature to allow him to be the man of the relationship and guide her in a place where she had always hoped to be in life. In Love and in complete joy being with him and in his arms.

This is a love that neither one of them had ever expected to come along let alone when they met that it would have happened to them. They are both in a place of pure joy and feeling the real aspect of what love is supposed to be about is a joy that they could have never imagined.

This man came along at a time in her life when she needed and wanted to have that kind of love. He was there for her when no one else could or would understand what she was going through in situations that came up.

He had been through his own hell. He had overcome many obstacles that people told him would not happen because he was living his life in the streets and never really taking the time to find love or be loved. Falling in love is a wonderful feeling to enjoy. My new love has given me so much joy and love in a short time. He brings a smile to my face every day by showing me how much he loves me. He tells me and then he shows me all the time. When you find someone in your life that is more focused on loving you and showing you how much you mean to them, that is a very special person. My husband is by best friend, he is my joy and my sunshine, he gives me happiness without even trying because he truly loves me. I have waited my entire life to have this type of love in my life and now to have it and share it with the world is just short of amazing. God gave me my greatest gift when he brought this man into my life. I am truly blessed.

The wake up for any of us is that when you fall in love with someone you are hoping that it will be forever. I feel like today is a new day and a different world, so we must keep our eyes open to the things going on around us and make sure that we don't get caught up in the fantasy. This is the time in your life that you are going to make sure that the things that you want out of life will be those things that are a right for you in the end.

About the Author

My name is Clara, I am a woman who grew up in Ohio, I am a daughter, mother, grandma, sister, cousin, aunt, friend, and most of all me. I spent most of my life there and spread my winds in 2012 to find a new me. I started on a journey to find myself and help others in the process of seeing that sometimes in life we have to find a piece of love in ourselves before we can find it in someone else. This book is just a part of me of my life as is the first two that I wrote. The goal here is to show others that they are strong and beautiful and can do anything that they put their minds to achieve as you as you never give up. Age is nothing but a number, you are never too old to strive for greatness... God bless